Then, all time stopped.

Fantasy(ファンタジー)

초판 1쇄 인쇄　2024년 10월 02일
초판 1쇄 발행　2024년 10월 18일

신고번호　제313-2010-376호
등록번호　105-91-58839

지은이　Lee Hu(李後)

발행처　보민출판사
발행인　김국환
기획　　김선희
편집　　소예늘
디자인　김민정

ISBN　979-11-6957-234-7　　03840

주소　경기도 파주시 해울로 11, 우미린더퍼스트@ 상가 2동 109호
전화　070-8615-7449
사이트　www.bominbook.com

- This book is a work protected by copyright law, so unauthorized reproduction is prohibited.
- 本書は著作権法で保護された著作物であるため、無断転載は禁止されています。

Fantasy

Lee Hu(李後)

Time passed by like a flash

Autobiography

One day, while walking down the street, I heard a love song. I stopped walking for no reason and stood there in silence until the song ended.

It must have been around that time. Since that day, I often thought, 'How long is the shelf life of love? Does endless love really exist?' along with the melody that never left my head.

That's how this story began.

One day, at the age of thirty

Lee Hu

Table of Contents

Autobiography • 4

1. Lovesick ✦

As if I didn't know from the beginning • 10

A fleeting moment • 11

Cold • 13

Protecting • 14

A bold boast • 15

Our attitude toward dealing with separation • 16

I hope it doesn't end like this • 17

A wrestler's Love • 18

Pain • 19

Time's stillness 1 • 20

Time's stillness 2 • 21

Time's stillness 3 • 22

Habit • 23

I had a sad dream • 24

Without resting • 26

After the rain, it's clear • 28

It's already like this • 29

Everyday 1 • 30

Everyday 2 • 31

To the distant you in my memories • 32

I want to stop • 33

I decided to do that • 34

So I, • 35

And yet, you still • 36

Where are you • 37

Unbearable • 38

Lovesick 1 • 39

Lovesick 2 • 40

Fade Out • 41

2. Like a Novel ✦

Winter Rain • 44

Waiting • 46

Tearful Latte • 47

But One Thing Is Certain • 48

Speed Dial 1 • 49

Love Letter • 50

Spring • 52

Like Watching a Sad Movie • 53

3. Comfort ✦

10 Years Later • 58

Just laugh • 59

Young Face 1 • 60

Young Face 2 • 61

London Smog • 62

As If It's the Last • 63

Unknown • 64

Undefined Direction • 65

Thirty, Winter • 66

Without • 67

Women are always sad • 68

Comfort • 69

Ideal • 70

Can't sleep • 71

Rejected by a third party • 72

Important things • 74

Boring • 75

Always cheerful • 76

Hope • 78

4. Terrible love ✦

Like her, he too • 80

Like your wind • 82

A practice of memory • 83

Late regret • 84

You won't know • 85

Don't be sorry • 86

I didn't send it • 87

I love you, but I won't love you • 89

Delete • 90

If your heart is much bigger than you think • 92

A sad song or a sad story • 94

A sad breakup • 95
If you look at it from a different perspective • 96
We'll meet someday • 97
The old garden • 98
Clean up • 99
Terrible love • 100
Resignation • 101
Chaos • 102
Parallel theory • 103
White out • 104

5. I missed you ✦

A warm person • 106
Slide to unlock • 107
I missed you • 108
Reject call • 109
Orpheus's heart • 110
Main Character 1 and Pedestrian 1 • 112

6. Fantasy ✦

I thought I could do that • 114
Let's make the separation beautiful • 115
Fantasy • 116

In summary • 117

1
Love Sick

As if I didn't know from the beginning | A fleeting moment | Cold | Protecting | A bold boast | Our attitude toward dealing with separation | I hope it doesn't end like this | A wrestler's Love | Pain | Time's stillness 1 | Time's stillness 2 | Time's stillness 3 | Habit | I had a sad dream | Without resting | After the rain, it's clear | It's already like this | Everyday 1 | Everyday 2 | To the distant you in my memories | I want to stop | I decided to do that | So I, | And yet, you still | Where are you | Unbearable | Lovesick 1 | Lovesick 2 | Fade Out

As if I never knew from the beginning

I take one step back.

Two steps, three steps, eleven steps, twelve steps away.

I will gradually move away and forget about it.

As if I never knew from the beginning.

A fleeting moment

In the boundless clear and transparent blue,
I draw you in it.
I never knew that longing was such a name for sadness.

'I love you.'
In a fleeting moment, I breathe in my heart and call your name.

'Have I ever hugged you warmly?'
No, I have received so much from you, but I have not done anything for you.

I liked you, but I never expressed my love properly,
and foolishly
I wait for you like this, regretting it later.

While moving to countless places, when will we run into each other by chance?
If we do, what kind of expression should I make?
A few hours pass and you are nowhere to be seen.
Of course, you must have passed by here briefly today, or maybe not.
If someone sees me, they might point a finger and say, 'Am I wasting my time on useless emotional consumption?'
But I want to say.

The fleeting moment of thinking of her is the greatest happiness for me

Cold

I can't continue speaking because I'm so sad,
and my throat is choked up.

I can't make a sound at that sad name called you.

Protecting

Love with your heart, not your head,

I feel so bad when I think of you living fiercely in a society

that is like a battlefield where the weak eat the strong.

I want to protect you until the end.

I want to protect you and love you,

with everything I can do,

until my energy runs out.

I want to protect you and love you with all my heart.

With all I have,

You

A bold boast

"Oppa, isn't that star pretty? That star is your star, and the star that twinkles next to your star is my star."
"I can pick all the stars in the sky for you."
He continues to talk to the woman with loving eyes.
"If you marry me later, I'll make sure not a drop of water gets on your fingertips."

There's nothing he can't say if he wants to get married.
He keeps talking like that.

Our attitude toward dealing with separation

"We have to get used to separation. You will experience many separations in the future."
But this time is also temporary, this moment will pass and somewhere else.

If there is a meeting, there will be a separation. That is natural. Therefore, there is absolutely no need to be sad about separation.
Because as time passes, we will be forgotten in each other's memories.

I hope it doesn't end like this

There's a song about sad love on the radio right now.
As I listen to the song, I quietly close my eyes and think of you.

You and I are at a distance where I can't meet you,
where I can't meet you or see you anymore.
When I quietly close my eyes, you're right in front of my eyes.
Your bright smile remains in my heart and doesn't seem to leave.
I love you.

I hope it doesn't end like this

A Wrestler's Love

"Your ears are like dumplings. You're so cute."
Where is she who used to clap her hands and laugh and what is she doing now?
How hard must it have been to live as a wrestler?
Was the decision he made the right one?

He can't forget the woman who loved him even in his weaknesses
And today, without fail, he drinks a glass of soju at a street food stall.

Pain

My heart was torn to pieces, but I couldn't let you go.

I love you so much.

Even when you don't think of me, always stay by my side…….

Time's stillness 1

I love you.

Even in those times when you don't think of me.

Time's stillness 2

'I wish this moment of thinking of you would stop like this.'

The man looked on indifferently and thought.

Then, all time stopped.

Even the act of wandering around to find a time he didn't know about.

Time's stillness 3

She put her earphones in her ears, closed her eyes, and listened to music.

Then, all time seemed to have stopped and it was quiet.

She wished that this time of thinking of him would stop like this.

She dreamed of him.

Love confined her to her emotions, excluding rational judgment.

In front of the time that passed so indifferently,

she said once again, 'It's okay.'

Habit

Again, like a habit,

Thinking of you.

I had a sad dream

The moment he said, "You were everything to me," the boy woke up from his dream.

Every day, without rest, I think of you, so I meet you in my dreams.

My heart doesn't change, and I don't give my heart easily, like this.

Most people interpret things in a way that is favorable to them, and they only see, hear, and believe what they want.

I can always press number 1, but I can't because, while it may be romance to me, it may be something shockingly terrible to you.

Then I think I'll be really sad.

The reality of not being able to see you or hear your voice is so sad.

Are you living each day forgetting?

I live each day remembering clearly.

There was no beginning, so there will be no end.

But my heart, I want to wait for you always.

I want to live each day like that, counting the days until we meet again.

I want to hold your hand and start anew on the day we meet again.

That's why I don't want to say it's over or that I've left.

My heart, my heart towards you, is still there, not leaving.

I didn't know that I was such a tearful person,

or that I was so weak-hearted and fragile.

Without resting

You are in my dreams every day.
Should I touch my phone and send a text message?
After sending a text message,
I will want to talk on the phone,
and after talking on the phone, I will want to meet you and see your face.
Thoughts are endless.
Anyone who has ever loved someone alone will know.
The fact that you can't stop yourself from being selfish and putting your feelings first regardless of the other person's wishes, even though you know it's not good.

"If you love, you have to love."
As if it were a promise, I can hear the heroine's voice from somewhere.

I can't stop this feeling that I can't control.
'I can do it well, I'm confident that I can cherish and love you more than anyone else.'

Those words that stop in my thoughts and linger in my mouth,
I can't stop them.

After the rain, it' clear

No matter how much you think about it, what can't be helped can't be helped.
After the rain comes the clear.
It will be like that someday.
So I hope my heart will be at ease.
What should I do now?

It's already like this

Suddenly, looking at the calendar, I think, May is over, and my heart flutters.

'It's already Friday. Already!'

Time passes by like this without me even thinking about it.

Already like this

I'm still living in that time

Everyday 1

'Now, wherever I am, I only think of you.'

If I can't even think about it, I can't stand it.
The time that I didn't allow passes by without a care

Everyday 2

I miss you so much that I can barely stand it.

Now you have become everything to me,

To you

To the distant you in my memories

A shower came down in the middle of the night, and while   I was drinking, I suddenly started thinking of you again, out of habit.
The words I haven't said yet,

To you, far away in my memory.

I want to stop

I'll live like that, crying and laughing

If I can't forget like that, then I can't help it

I can't stand the small victory inside me.

If I could go back to the time before I didn't know you,

I want to just pass by then.

I want to stop.

I decided to do that

I thought about it again, but I couldn't come to a conclusion.

I think I'll think about it a lot tomorrow and the day after.

After pressing the stop button, I lay down.

Without any preparation,

I decided to do that.

So I,

'How can I love deeply?'

While reading a book, the thought suddenly occurred to me.

I think of her several times a day, dozens of times, and call her name.

Was the depth of my love really this deep?

When that thought suddenly occurred to me, I went out to the streets to look for her.

I waited helplessly, not knowing where she was or what she was doing.

But she was nowhere to be found.......

So I wanted to call you.

And yet, you still

Still, you are still, my love.

Even though you are indifferent to me, the smile I used to love is still the same

My love is by my side

Now, when I close my eyes, I can feel it.

I lived all day long only loving, so it's okay.

My heart.

Someday, after a short time

I can communicate with you again,

I can smile happily and meet you again,

I hope that day will come.......

Then, then, I will give you all the love I have

Where are you

He was nowhere.

I thought about the distance he might have walked,

I sat in the same place he might have sat,

I recalled the conversations we had.

I sat quietly, taking a sip of cherry ade,

It felt as if he was sitting next to me.

His warm smile that smiled brightly at me…….

While I was repeating to myself, 'You were everything to me,'

As if I was dreaming, Iruma's 'River flows in you' was flowing out of my earphones.

Maybe I was in that kind of love that had no end.

Unbearable

The words that imprison me in an inexplicable way.

From me.

Lovesick 1

867, Freedom of Mind, Bang Tae-won

8670, Sometimes, Britney Spears

86702, Lovesick, San E

Lovesick

Lovesick 2

As time passes, everything will disappear as if it was a dream.
As time passes, everything will be forgotten.
Even the memory that I promised to keep deep in my heart
Even the fact that I loved you

Fade Out

I close my eyes and listen to the music.

A lot of thoughts are tangled in my head.

Time flows along with the music, taking me back to that memory.

I was in a daze, forgetting what I was trying to say, and when I gathered my thoughts, the song was ending because I hadn't been able to press the return button.

Just as time once passed cannot be returned,

just as broken pieces of glass cannot be restored to their original state,

After the song ends, memories begin to move beyond the vanishing point.

Just like that,

just like this

the memories disappear from memory.

Fade Out.

Just a little closer, by my side…….

2
Like a novel

Winter Rain | Waiting | Tearful Latte | But One Thing Is Certain | Speed Dial 1 | Love Letter | Spring | Like Watching a Sad Movie

Winter Rain

When I first saw you, I couldn't take my eyes off you.

The saying that you fall in love at first sight.

That saying that you fell in love at first sight. Before, I didn't believe in the stupid saying called 'fate'. However, I changed after meeting you.

I loved your voice, your face, and even the small breaths you let out every now and then, and I started to think of them as habits.

In front of a cafe that I found by following your voice. The song you liked was playing here. Was it because the atmosphere of the cafe was similar to your taste? Or was it because I heard the song you liked? I think I can hear your voice somewhere here and now.

I sat in a cafe with a familiar voice and a familiar melody, and in my fantasy, you were drinking mocha coffee and I was drinking a banana shake.

It felt familiar, like a kind of deja vu phenomenon that I had seen somewhere before. It was so comfortable, as if I had known you for a long time in the past.

Your warm gaze, your bright smile, and the beautiful stars twinkling in your clear eyes.

Yes, you are like a star that is unusually small and beautiful.

Did I ever tell you that?

Why, that memory will be erased from memory.

The day I first saw you, I thought it was fate. And I had a feeling that I would fall into a sad love and not be able to escape.

"No matter how many times you say and shout it, love is something that is eventually forgotten……. I will pray that you meet someone better than me and be happy."

Now, it has come to this with your request to forget.

In the end, it has become a sad love story that must be forgotten from memory.

'Forgetting is a really sad thing.'

Waiting

Even though I know that the end of that blind and one-sided love can never be beautiful,
I am waiting.
If only I can see it just once.

Tearful Latte

Man: I wish this moment, looking at you, would last forever.

Woman: Yes?

Man: (Looking at woman with sad eyes) Always by your side, always, stay.

Stop Motion stops the situation and switches to black and white screen.
Time seems to have stopped, and the surroundings are quiet.

But One Thing is Certain

The night deepens.

No words, no expressions, only unrefined thoughts remain.

1, 2, 3, 4, 5, 6, 7, 8, 9, 10, 11, 12, 13, 14, 15, 16, 17, 18, 19, 20

After 20 seconds, sensations arise.

However, unrefined sensations do not develop introspection.

The same goes for things that stop in thoughts.

Speed Dial 1

He still couldn't stop thinking.

The only thing he could do whenever he wanted to see her was to write her name all over a white piece of paper and think of her.

He wrote her name all over the white piece of paper, 'Lee Keut-soon, Lee Keut-soon.'

And then, 'Dreuruk', his cell phone vibrated.

The cell phone gave him valuable information, saying, 'Today, you can borrow 10 million won.'

He looked at his cell phone and thought of speed dial number 1.

It was the only way to communicate with her, and at the same time, it had great meaning.

He recalled it all in a moment from his memory.

Love Letter

Erased and rewritten, erased and rewritten again.

I did it because I still had regrets. And the whispers that I couldn't contain inside me,

Now distant in my memories, old stories have become sad melodies, wrapping around my body, shaking up my daily life, and continuing to travel one way without stopping.

One night, when the words I wanted to say were returned, I had a dream. In that dream, I was wandering around looking for you.

"Where are you now? Where are you and what are you doing? Are you doing well? Are you eating well, sleeping well, and living like that? I wonder. Everything." I was shouting like that in a place where there was no one or nothing.

When did it start? When did I start thinking about you?

Were the words I said to you not sincere, or was it because my love wasn't earnest?

Spring

Until the influence of the Yangtze River air mass.

After the influence of the Siberian air mass ends,

Before the influence of the North Pacific and Okhotsk Sea air masses.

The first season when dividing a year into four seasons, Spring.

Like Watching a Sad Movie

I loved too much.

So, I gave up everything.

Even I,

I've endured it well so far.

I can handle it.

Now…….

"Love is pain. Love is really painful. When I wake up from a dream that can't come true, the fact that I'm alone in the room makes my heart ache. A love that makes my heart feel empty and like it's going to burst at any moment. Especially, in the case of blind and one-sided love. He got to know a woman and fell in love with her. One day, he sat across from her and drank a beverage and talked. He thought about how beautifully he remembered and dreamed of that moment, and whether a moment like this would come again, whether such moments would come to him. Everything is just a dream for a moment, and the words that lock him up are also just a moment, and the words that pass by are only for that moment……. Let's love, it hurts. One day, he looked back at himself and realized that he had nothing to say to her, and he could see his shabby and miserable self after taking a shower and rubbing the steamy mirror with his palm. He wanted to give up everything. He wanted to run away somewhere far away. He wished that the time he spent thinking about her would stop in his heart and that time would last forever. That's how it is, love is……. It's not love if you love someone, hold their hand, and lightly kiss them. Even if you sincerely wish for that person to do well, and you can't sit facing that person and laugh and talk, even if you smile happily all day thinking about that person and then dream of an impossible dream and feel sad again, that's love. Even if it's all settled someday, I wish this moment would last forever. If only it could……. It's not wrong for a person to like someone. In the end, it's okay because I lived all day loving even if it didn't come true. I can't control my feelings. Love confines him, excluding rational judgment and being swayed by emotions. Yes, he was trapped in a prison called 'love'. When time passes like a passing wind, it will be okay. He, who cannot even handle his feelings, is now trying to sort them out. At the time, it was really heartbreaking and sad, but when it actually passes, it will all be nothing, right? If he swallows a sleeping pill and water, he will fall asleep. When he wakes up, his heart will be at ease as if nothing had happened, as if nothing had happened. For a boy in puberty, love, like a fever, is also a season. If it doesn't turn out that way even though he believed it, there's nothing he can do about it. One day, he was walking down the street and saw clothes displayed in a shop window and thought, 'They're really pretty. These clothes would suit her.' No, at that time, he bought her those clothes in his head. She put them on and spun around, smiling brightly at him. But, it was all just imagination. The woman he had with him was nowhere to be found. Everything was a dream for a moment, and the ending credits were rolling on the screen in the theater. "It's so heartbreaking and sad, as if I've just watched a sad movie."

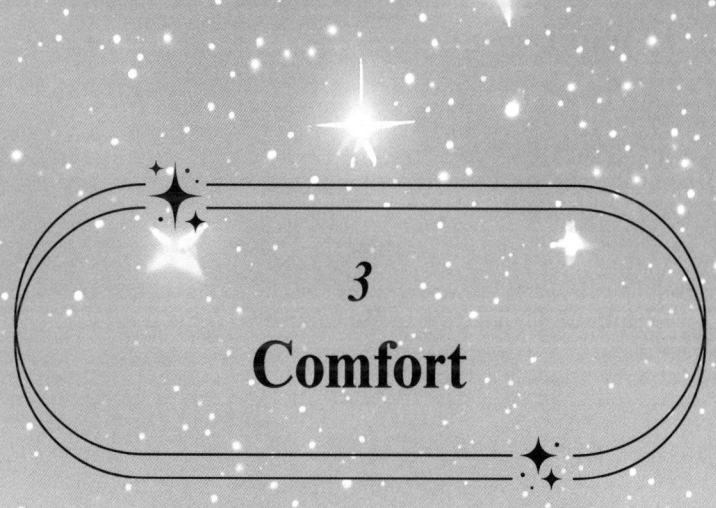

3
Comfort

10 Years Later | Just laugh | Young Face 1 | Young Face 2 | London Smog | As If It's the Last | Unknown | Undefined Direction | Thirty, Winter | Without | Women are always sad | Comfort | Ideal | Can't sleep | Rejected by a third party | Important things | Boring | Always cheerful | Hope

10 Years Later

"Thank you for applying to our company. Can you tell us about yourself in 10 years?"

"Yes. I want to be a managing director of this company in 10 years. Open parenthesis, alcohol, close parenthesis, managing director."

(Alcohol) Managing Director

Just laugh

Just laugh.

Young Face 1

"Born in 1982, I'm thirty this year."

"Oh, really? You look young. You don't look that young."

"Thank you. I look young. How old do I look?"

"Born in January 1983, I'm twenty-nine."

Young Face 2

"Hey, I'm 40 this year. How old do I look?"

"Really? You look young."

"How old do you look?"

"15, a middle school freshman who repeated a year."

London Smog

Our 50-year-old lady, how much trouble did you have after giving birth to me at the age of 21?

To quote the expression of comedian Kim Gu-ra, my eldest son's current situation is like the London smog, and the sky is cloudy.

I can't see anything right now.

The number of unemployed young people is approaching 1.2 million, and I'm competing with high-spec people in a place where they are abundant.

But don't worry too much.

Your eldest son has the tenacity to survive even if you drop him on a deserted island.

It's called hardship and suffering.

Now that the difficult times have passed, just think about the bright future that lies ahead.

As If It's the Last

After taking the graduation exam,

my college life is actually over.

I wonder when I will ever come back to school.

After moving around here and there, I have arrived at the final destination.

Studying hard, hanging out with many people,

and moving forward with passion for something

It feels like it was just a dream, and I feel both regretful and bittersweet.

As if it were the last.

Unknown

There are so many things in the world that I don't know even though I know them.

I wonder what will happen in the future, what kind of properties they will have.

I don't know.

I don't know.

Undecided Direction

"What are you going to do in the future?"

Kang-gyu asked.

"I don't know right now. Nothing has been decided yet, but well, right now I'm just vaguely looking ahead. But I can go anywhere."

I answered.

Thirty, Winter

Time doesn't wait for me,

and I turn thirty without any preparation.

Without

Without any more pain and sorrow…….

I wish I could live like that.

Women are always sad

The woman said,

"I want to receive a letter from you."

Then, without a moment's hesitation, the man writes a letter and places it in the woman's thin, white hands.

The woman, who received the rough letter that was neither neat nor had any scent, reads it out loud in front of the man.

"Anyone who reads this letter must send the same message to 100 people within 24 hours……."

"You don't know love."

The woman said.

Comfort

Don't all job seekers feel similar emotions?

At first, I thought I could do well, but I was exhausted by the constant failures, and it's been a long time since I've seen my friends, and it's been a long time since I've put my TOEIC book down, and I'm just lying around feeling helpless and inferior, or going for a walk nearby.

Yes, youth without pain is not remembered as youth.

I hope that one day, Merry J will be able to recall this moment with a smile.

Ideal

A life that is not bound by worldly things,
and is content with small things and knows how to be grateful

However, reality and ideals are far apart.

Can't sleep

I can't sleep.

I wander through the dark maze where lies swallow the truth.

Rejected by a third party

He asked her.

"What kind of car do you drive? You should drive at least a mid-sized car. It's a bit awkward to ask about your annual salary when we first meet. I think I can guess your annual salary by looking at your car."

"Yes, I use public transportation. I walk a lot. I walk a lot, so I'm called a 'walker.'"

"Then, where do you work? Oh, salary is more important than the company. How much does Mirae earn? After all, material things are reality. Oh, and tell me about your academic background. I'd also like to know your TOEIC score, but I think it's rude to ask for it. If you tell me, I'll take note."

"I'm just playing around right now, so I don't have any income. My highest level of education is a night school graduate. Oh, but I do have a TOEIC score. It's around

100. But why are you asking me this?"

"Mirae doesn't have a future. Unfortunately, you don't have the conditions to make friends with me. If you have any feelings for my friend, please hurry up and get over it and continue on your way. Fighting."

She was dumped by a third party who had no feelings at all and was not even the person involved.

That evening, Mirae was laughing out loud while watching a funny comedy show without thinking about anything. It was an evening where only the popcorn melting in her mouth seemed to know her feelings.

Important things

Everyone has probably thought about it at least once.

Am I falling behind others?

Because I have bad grades, or my language skills are bad, or I am not confident about my appearance, or I started my studies late and am old, or I do not have any significant career, etc.

But that is not the important issue. You can start late.

What is more important is not where I am now,

but what I have set as my goal and where I am going.

I wonder if I have set the right direction for my life.

Am I missing out on what is really important right now?

'Where am I going now?'

Bored

"Oh, I'm bored. How long do I have to listen to young people's love stories? I'm bored. I'm bored."

"I'm bored."

Always cheerful

At this point, there should definitely be a lot of worries and concerns about employment or future issues, but I don't feel or have any feelings at all.

Nothing has been decided, is in progress, or is progressing.

Is it because I live without thinking?

Yes, that's because I live without thinking.

But it might be better to do this now than to worry about something in the future that hasn't happened yet.

After all, good things are good.

I stopped by a flower shop while walking down the street, and while smelling the flowers, I asked the florist, "The flowers smell really good. What's the name of the flower?"

And the owner said, "That's an artificial flower."

I guess he mistook the smell for a slight cold.

These days, I laugh at trivial things like this.

Yes, if I keep laughing like this, good days will come

someday, I guess.

I like not being sad more than being sad.

Hope

It's still dark and dim

But someday a warm spring will come

Yes, someday a good day will come

With that hope

I believe this moment will be a memory that I will remember with a smile…….

4
Terrible love

Like her, he too | Like your wind | A practice of memory | Late regret | You won't know | Don't be sorry | I didn't send it | I love you, but I won't love you | Delete | If your heart is much bigger than you think | A sad song or a sad story | A sad breakup | If you look at it from a different perspective | We'll meet someday | The old garden | Clean up | Terrible love | Resignation | Chaos | Parallel theory | White out

Like her, he too

"It's okay. Everything will be okay."

She said, embracing him with her warm hands. But sadly, a bomb exploded in his mind and everything disappeared like a mirage.

When he opened his eyes in surprise and looked at his wristwatch, cold sweat was running down his ears.

He let out a sigh of relief again and lay down again.

Another reality in the dream seemed like a deja vu phenomenon.

When he checked his time in his mind, an unreasonable sadness was weighing on his chest. Then, she wiped away his sad tears and said, "It's okay. Everything will be okay."

Then, everything disappeared like white dust.

As if in a dream, eons of time had passed without him knowing.

The moment his eyes, which had found stability, trembled

and began to see light, she was looking at him and feeling sad.

He held her with his warm hands and said, "It's okay. Everything will be okay." And said.

Like your wind

It was a hot summer.
I turned on the fan,
and stood in front of the fan, making sounds like 'Ah, ah, ah'.

Every time the natural wind touched my face,
I said 'Ah, ah, ah'

Ah, I quietly closed my eyes and felt the natural wind
and naturally, no, slowly and gradually, I forgot you.
As you wished
Like your wind

A practice of memory

A love that once seemed unbearable,

will break up and become strangers

and become strangers

and the day will come when it will be forgotten as if

nothing had happened between the two

Late regret

'I wanted to say that I liked you a lot for a long time, but it didn't work out well.'

You won't know

Do you know? No, you don't know. You don't want to know. You can't know my heart that's about to burst at any moment.

Don't be sorry

But I'm not even disappointed.
In this heart, in front of love

Every time I walk down the rainy Myeongdong street, I think of you.
Love rides the rain
Love rides the music
Slow, slow, quick, quick
Slow, slow, quick, quick
And it's over.

'Don't be sorry. It's the love I started.'

I didn't send it

"The first monsoon rain of the year is pouring down in the southern region right now."

I suddenly thought of you while listening to the weather forecast on the radio.
The first monsoon rain fell on the day we broke up.

Everything inside me pours out with your thoughts,
and like the memory of that day disappearing

the memory is moving away from the vanishing point.
But your warm voice still lingers in my ears.
As if I didn't let you go from my mind even though you left me.

People say that forgetting only takes a moment.

I don't want to forget.

I want to keep it deep in my heart and cherish it.

I love you,
but I won't love you

I'd rather pour only half the wine. When the scent of the wine gently tickles my nostrils, then I can play a chanson. My mouth keeps getting dry, I can't stand it. je t'aime, my love. The story is already over, but let me feel just enough sadness to handle and just enough sadness to endure, so that I can start again. After a sip of wine, let me go now so that I won't be sad anymore.

Delete

Take a deep breath and exhale.

Take another deep breath and exhale.

Your whole body becomes relaxed and comfortable.

Your whole body becomes relaxed and comfortable.

Your whole body loses strength and becomes comfortable.

Now there is a white board in front of you.

A high-quality picture of the person you love appears on the white board.

The picture of the person becomes clearer and clearer.

Now an envelope of medicine to cure your sick heart appears on top of the picture of the person. As the image of this envelope of medicine becomes clearer, your sick heart disappears.

Now, count to one, two, three and your sick heart will be healed.

One,

two,

three

Now your sick heart has been healed.

A blackboard eraser appears in front of the blackboard.

Use the blackboard eraser to erase the picture of the person you love little by little.

Now, count to one, two, three and the picture of the person will be erased white.

One,

two,

three

Now the picture of the person is erased and is gone.

Your heart becomes much lighter.

Your heart becomes much lighter and more comfortable.

Your heart becomes comfortable.

If your heart is much bigger than you think

I can't live like this anymore.
Even if I empty my heart, it will quickly fill up again.

I am to you,
You are to me,

A mosaic of memories is like a single photograph, a memory.

After countless hours, memories will fade into darkness.
I wish I could live like that without any more pain and sadness.......

I don't know. There's nothing I can do about it then.
If your heart is much bigger than you think, there's nothing I can do about it then.

I can't handle it.

I can't live like this anymore.

I'm filled with thoughts of you several times a day,

If your heart is much bigger than you think, there's nothing I can do about it then.

If your heart is much bigger than you think.

A sad song or a sad story

When I hear a sad story that has never been told in a storybook, or when I hear a singer's voice in a sad melody that I have only just heard for the first time,
At that time, I think of you.

A sad breakup

'I wish this was all a dream. I love you so much. I love you. I love you so much. I love you from head to toe. I love you. I love you. I love you so much. I love you from head to toe. I wish we could smile and talk again the day after we broke up,' I thought, but it didn't happen. You probably couldn't always do that. I wanted to protect and love you with all of my heart. There were so many things I wanted to do, but I'm sorry I couldn't.

'I wish this was all a dream.'
But do you know how I want you to look back at least once? Or do you pretend not to know even though you do? If you feel the same way, just smile and hug me as if nothing happened, as if nothing happened. Even if you're sad, don't be sad.

'I can't watch sad stories anymore.'

If you look at it from a different perspective

To buy you a cup of Starbucks coffee, I have to drill 500 holes in iron with a drill machine at the factory.

To buy you a cup of Coffee Bean coffee, I have to tighten 1,000 bolts at the factory.

I want to win your heart even if it means tightening, cleaning, and oiling.

"Who likes someone who does this?"
"No, don't think like that. There are so many people in this world who can't even make a living. Even so, Cheol-yeong, don't you have the means to drive a mid-sized car? In this world, where is the distinction between noble and base jobs? If you earn honestly without harming others and save frugally, that's the best."

We'll meet someday

"Honey, what were you doing?"

"I was thinking of you."

"Honey, what were you doing?"

"I was thinking of you. I should go to bed now. Let's hang up."

"Honey, when are we going to meet?"

"We'll meet someday."

"Honey, can we meet tomorrow?"

"I'm busy tomorrow."

"What about the day after tomorrow?"

"I'm busy the day after tomorrow, too."

"Then, what about the day after tomorrow?"

"I'm busy the day after tomorrow."

"Then when are we going to meet?"

"We'll meet someday, okay."

"I'll wait."

The old garden

After ordering an Americano at a coffee shop, I looked out the window and saw someone who looked like you. I wanted to see you again and again, "Is that the only woman in the world? Just forget about it now." I got angry without realizing it when my friend tried to comfort me and told me to just forget about it now. I covered my ears and didn't want to hear anything. Now, no matter where I am, all I can think about is you. "Did you like Americano?" I did. I probably did. The shift in my thoughts from certainty to uncertainty reminded me that I was forgetting you, and at that time, I couldn't do anything because my heart was aching and I didn't know what I was feeling. It's been a long time. It's been a long time. Old memories. Old sorrow, old forgetting, old memories. Every time I drink Americano, I think of you. Now, you've become everything inside me, and since I can't forget you, I'll just love you.

Clean up

"It's okay. If you think you hate me, just tell me honestly. Of course, it'll hurt, but I'll do it. I'll just empty my mind……."

Terrible love

Love and love, laugh at love, be heartbroken by love, smile at love, be sad at love, cry and laugh at love, love again, be sad and be hurt by love, be happy and love again and be sad again.

Ah, terrible love.

Resignation

It's really disgusting, dirty, deadly, and unjust.
When I was young, I didn't know that life was this difficult and hard.

But what can I do?
Well, I guess I'll just have to live like that.

Chaos

I am trapped in the name of you, like a black hole, and hot emotions are burning inside me

I call this heart and emotion that I cannot control,
Chaotic love

Please call me with 10 decibels added to my voice

It's confusing.
Everything,
Everything,
This emotion that must destroy the moment I decided to love for the rest of my life.

Parallel theory

No matter how many times I die and am reborn, I know that I will love you again in the end. We will meet again in an infinite orbit in countless cases. We will meet again and love each other as if it were fate in a different appearance and a different time. Just as the north pole of a magnet seeks the south pole, my heart will seek you. So it's okay. We are now separated and living like this without knowing each other's well-being.

Now we don't call, we don't send text messages, and we don't even feel heartbroken by the feverish love.

△ ▼ ▼ △ ∞∞∞∞ ≒ △ ▼ ▼ △ ∞∞∞∞∞
 ..   .   .
10438+139 23404

White Out

I'll be going around in circles again.

No matter how hard I try, I can't see you with the senses I've lost.

I'll be wandering far away even though I've kept you close.

Blinded by love, with your pure white heart.

Again, again, once more like this.

I'll lose my heart,

Time stops,

You disappear from my memories,

Love passes, memories disappear in the white snow.

Forgetting, losing, forgetting, losing, being forgotten.

I'll find my place again.

5
I missed you

A warm person | Slide to unlock | I missed you | Reject call | Orpheus's heart | Main Character 1 and Pedestrian 1

A warm person

After drawing the curtains and opening the window, dazzling sunlight came into the room.
The man thought.
'You were a dazzling person to me. Thank you. Thank you. You were such a warm person to me.'

Push to unlock

One day, when my mind was at ease,

I remember you

[Push to unlock]

I missed you

"I missed you."

Reject call

After hesitating, the woman calls the man.

'I was always one step behind you, but can you never see me? If you look at me, if you wave at me, I will always love you.'

As the cool ringing of the phone, composed of a part of Loveholic's music, disappears from her ears, the message, "The customer is not answering the phone right now."

The woman presses the end button with her slender index finger and mutters to herself, 'I shouldn't do that anymore.'

It was the moment when the woman's love ended.

Orpheus's heart

You are my love

You are my destiny

You are my sorrow

I would do anything for you.

Blinded by love,

My heart still stands still.

From the first time I met you until now.

Stay in my heart.

Then I will play the harp for you.

You close your eyes and listen to the song I composed.

That all this is but a dream,

When this song ends and you open your eyes,

Everything in this song will disappear in an instant.

Yes, that is how dreamers are.

It seems that I will not be able to write any more songs or

words with these hands.

But you are still my love,

My destiny.

I will love you with all that I have.

Main Character 1 and Pedestrian 1

The second-best boobies among Hongdae club lovers, the main character 1, proposed to Pedestrian 1 by giving her a jewel candy ring (jewel candy) as a penalty for losing a game called 'Baskin Robbins 31' in front of New York Bakery, which is about a 5-minute walk from Exit 6 of Gangnam Station.

Pedestrian 1 accepted the proposal of someone she had only known for 3 minutes, and they got married and lived happily ever after.

6
Fantasy

I thought I could do that | Let's make the separation beautiful | Fantasy

I thought I could do that

"Do you know what earnestness is? It was really earnest. If it had to be a heartbreaking heartache, I would be happy to be hurt a thousand times, ten thousand times. I thought how great it would be if I could do that just for one moment, just once. If it had to hurt that much, then there was a day when I thought I could do it."

Let's make the separation beautiful

#. 1126611

BGM: Love me by Yiruma

A man and a woman meet at the midpoint of Ojakgyo Bridge in Gwanghanru, Namwon-si, Jeollabuk-do.

Man: I really meant it. My heart fluttered and I was happy every time I thought of Chunhyang. Thank you.

Woman: My heart aches so much when I think of having to break up with Mongryong. I was happy that you treated me warmly, despite my infinite shortcomings. Thank you.

Fantasy

There is a man in front of the mirror.

In the man's eyes, I see the time that was not allowed.

I don't want to tell you all the details of the fantasy that unfolded in time.

It's too bad.

I feel like I won't be able to see you again once I open that door.

It's time to wake up from the fantasy.

It's time to say goodbye.

Goodbye.

In summary

It is clear that only by matching the rhyme, syllable, and melody and bringing out the rhythm can the value of poetry be increased. However, I tried to think in a different direction. Should I say that forcing it together felt like mechanically stamping out something? I wanted to escape from the monotony of no change. So I tried to express it as it was, just as I first felt it.

I wanted to think in a new way. I couldn't rely on analog thinking forever. In addition to writing down the thoughts that came to my mind with a pen on a memo pad, I also wanted to capture emotions that are easy to miss by using the voice recording function of my smartphone.

I try to look at everything in a new way in order to write more vivid writing. From the moment I open my eyes in the morning until I fall asleep at night, I try to think like a writer and act like a writer. Even when I eat, I eat like a writer.

I call this a new thought and change. Even now, the paradigm is changing within the Möbius strip in my head.

And the whole story ended in my memory.

そして、すべての時間が止まりました。

ファンタジー

李虎（リー・フー）

すれ違った時間

自伝

ある日、道を歩いていると、ラブソングが聞こえてきました。何の理由もなく立ち止まり、歌が終わるまで黙って立っていました。

その頃だったと思います。その日から、頭から離れないメロディーとともに、「愛の賞味期限はどれくらいなんだろう？ 終わりのない愛は本当に存在するんだろうか？」とよく考えるようになりました。

それがこの物語の始まりです。

ある日、30歳の時

李虎

目次

自伝・122

1. 恋煩い ✦

初めから知らなかったかのように・128
つかの間の瞬間・129
冷たさ・131
守る・132
はったり・133
別れに対する私たちの態度・134
こんなふうに終わらなければいいのに・135
レスラーの愛・136
痛み・137
時間を止める 1・138
時間を止める 2・139
時間を止める 3・140
習慣・141
悲しい夢を見た・142
休むことなく・144
雨の後は晴れ・146
もうこうやって・147
毎日 1・148
毎日 2・149
記憶の中の遠いあなたへ・150
やめたい・151

やることにした・152
それで私は、・153
それでも、あなたはまだ・154
どこにいるの・155
耐えられない何か・156
恋煩い 1・157
恋煩い 2・158
フェードアウト・159

2. 小説のように ✦

冬の雨・162
私は待っています・164
ティアラテ・165
しかし、一つだけ確かなことは・166
短縮ダイヤル 1・167
ラブレター・168
春・169
悲しい映画を見ているよう・170

3. 慰め ✦

10年後・174
ただ笑う・175
若い顔 1・176
若い顔 2・177
ロンドンのスモッグ・178
まるで最後みたい・179

知らないこと・180
未定の方向・181
30歳、冬・182
なし・183
だから女はいつも悲しんでいる・184
安らぎ・185
理想・186
眠れない・187
第三者に拒否されました・188
重要・190
退屈だ・191
いつも明るい・192
希望・194

4. ひどい愛 ✦

彼女と同じように、彼も・196
君の風のように・198
記憶の練習・199
後になって後悔・200
知らない・201
後悔しないで・202
送ってないよ・203
愛しているけど、愛さない・205
削除・206
もし君の心が君が思っているよりもずっと大きいのなら・208
悲しい歌や悲しい物語・210
悲しい別れ・211
見方を変えれば・213

いつか会おうね・214
昔の庭・215
片付けなさい・216
ひどい愛・217
諦め・218
混沌・219
平行理論・220
ホワイトアウト・221

5. 会いたかったよ ✦

温かい人・224
プッシュしてロックを解除・225
会いたかったよ・226
電話を拒否・227
オルフェウスの心・228
主人公１と歩行者１・230

6. ファンタジー ✦

私にはそれができる・232
別れは美しく・233
ファンタジー・234

まとめ・235

1
恋煩い

初めから知らなかったかのように｜つかの間の瞬間｜冷たさ｜守る｜はったり｜別れに対する私たちの態度｜こんなふうに終わらなければいいのに｜レスラーの愛｜痛み｜時間を止める1｜時間を止める2｜時間を止める3｜習慣｜悲しい夢を見た｜休むことなく｜雨の後は晴れ｜もうこうやって｜毎日1｜毎日2｜記憶の中の遠いあなたへ｜やめたい｜やることにした｜それで私は、｜それでも、あなたはまだ｜どこにいるの｜耐えられない何か｜恋煩い1｜恋煩い2｜フェードアウト｜もう少し近く

初めから知らなかったかのように

一歩後退します。

2歩、3歩、11歩、12歩と離れます。

徐々に離れて忘れていきます。

まるで最初から知らなかったかのように。

つかの間の瞬間

限りなく澄んだ青に、
君を引き寄せる。
憧れが悲しみの名だなんて知らなかった。

「君を愛している」
つかの間のひととき、胸に息を吸い込み、君の名前を呼ぶ。

「君を温かく抱きしめたことはあるか？」
いいえ、君からたくさんのことをもらったけれど、君のために何もしてあげられなかった。

君が好きだったけれど、ちゃんと愛情を伝えられず、
愚かにも
こうして君を待って、後悔している。
数え切れない場所を移動しながら、いつ偶然出会うのだろ

う。
出会ったらどんな表情をすればいいのだろう。
数時間が経っても君の姿はどこにもない。
もちろん、今日はここを少し通り過ぎたに違いない、あるいはそうでないかもしれない。
誰かが私を見たら、指をさして「無駄な感情の消費に時間を浪費しているの？」と言うかもしれない。
でも、言いたい。

彼女のことを思う束の間のひとときが私にとって最高の幸せです。

冷たさ

悲しくて喉が詰まって話し続けられない。

君を呼ぶ悲しい名前に声も出ない。

守る

頭ではなく心で愛する、
弱肉強食の戦場のような社会で激しく生きる君のことを考えると、とてもつらい気持ちになる。
最後まで君を守りたい。
全力で君を守り、愛したい、
僕のエネルギーが尽きるまで。

心を尽くして君を守り、愛したい。
僕のすべてをかけて、
君を

はったり

「お兄ちゃん、あの星きれいじゃない？ あの星は君の星、君の星の隣で輝く星は僕の星だよ。」
「空にある星を全部選んであげるよ。」
彼は愛情に満ちた目で女性に話しかけ続ける。
「後で僕と結婚してくれたら、指先に水が一滴もかからないようにしてあげるよ。」

結婚したいなら、言えないことは何もない。
彼はそう言い続ける。

別れに対する私たちの態度

「別れには慣れなければなりません。これから先、たくさんの別れを経験するでしょう。」
しかし、この時間も一時的なもので、この瞬間は過ぎ去り、どこか別の場所へ移ります。

出会いがあれば、別れもあります。それは自然なことです。ですから、別れを悲しむ必要はまったくありません。時間が経つにつれて、私たちはお互いの記憶から忘れ去られていくからです。

こんな風に終わらなければいいのに

今ラジオで悲しい恋の歌が流れている。
その歌を聴きながら、静かに目を閉じて君を思う。

君と私はもう会えない距離にいる。
もう君に会えないし、君を見ることもできない。
静かに目を閉じると、君は目の前にいる。
君の明るい笑顔は僕の心の中に残っていて、離れないようだ。
君を愛していた。

こんな風に終わらなければいいのに

レスラーの恋

「君の耳は餃子みたいだ。とても可愛いね。」
手を叩いて笑っていた彼女は今どこにいて何をしているのだろう？
レスラーとして生きるのはどれほど大変だったのだろう？
彼の決断は正しかったのだろうか？

彼は自分の弱さにも関わらず愛してくれた女性を忘れられず
そして今日も彼は必ず屋台で焼酎を一杯飲む。

痛み

私の心は引き裂かれましたが、あなたを手放すことはできませんでした。
私はあなたをとても愛しています。
あなたが私のことを考えていないときでも、いつも私のそばにいてください……。

時間を止める１

あなたを愛しています。
あなたが私のことを考えていないときでも。

時間を止める2

「君を想うこの瞬間が、このまま止まればいいのに。」
男は無関心に見つめながら考えた。
すると すべての時間が止まった。
知らない時間を探してさまようという行為さえも。

時間を止める3

彼女はイヤホンを耳に当て、目を閉じて音楽を聴いていた。
すると、すべての時間が止まったようで、静かになった。
彼女は、彼を想うこの時間がこのまま止まればいいのにと思った。
彼女は彼のことを夢に見た。
愛は彼女を感情に閉じ込め、理性的な判断を排除した。
無関心に過ぎていく時間の前で、
彼女はもう一度言った。「大丈夫。」

習慣

また習慣のように、
あなたのことを考えています

悲しい夢を見た

「君は僕にとってすべてだった。」と言った瞬間、少年は夢から覚めた。
毎日休むことなく君を想うから、夢の中で君に会う。
僕の心は変わらないし、簡単には心を許さない。
ほとんどの人は自分に都合のいいように物事を解釈し、自分の見たいこと、聞きたいこと、信じたいことだけを見る。
いつでも1番を押せるけど、僕にとっては恋愛でも、君にとっては衝撃的な恐ろしいことかもしれないから押せない。
そうなったら本当に悲しくなると思う。
君に会えない、声が聞けない現実がとても悲しい。
君は毎日忘れて生きてる?
僕は毎日はっきりと思い出しながら生きてる。
始まりがなかったから、終わりもない。
でも僕の心は、ずっと君を待ち続けたい。

また会う日まで数えながら、そんな風に毎日を生きたい。
また会う日に君の手を握って、新しく始めたい。
だから、もう終わったとか、私が去ったとか言いたくないんです。
私の心、あなたに対する私の心は、まだそこにあって、去っていません。

自分がこんなに涙もろい人間だとは、
知らなかったし、心が弱くて脆い人間だとも。

休む間もなく

君は毎日夢の中にいる。
携帯を触ってメールを送ろうか？
メールを送ったら電話で話したくなるし、電話をしたら君に会って顔を見たいと思う。
考えは尽きない。
一人で誰かを愛したことがある人なら誰でもわかるだろう。
良くないとわかっていても、相手の意向に関係なく自分の気持ちを優先し、自分勝手になってしまうことをやめられないこと。

「愛するなら愛さなければならない。」
まるで約束のように、どこからともなくヒロインの声が聞こえる。

自分では抑えられないこの気持ちを止めることができな

い。
「私はうまくやれる、誰よりも君を大切に愛せる自信がある。」

考えに止まり、口に残るその言葉、
止めることができない。

雨の後は晴れ

いくら考えても、どうしようもないことはどうしようもない。
雨の後は晴れ。
いつかはそうなる。
だから心が楽になればいい。
これからどうすればいい？

もうこうやって

ふとカレンダーを見ると、5月も終わってしまったんだな、と胸がときめく。
「もう金曜日だ。もう！」
何も考えずにこうやって時間が過ぎていく。
もうこうやって
私はまだその時間を生きている。

毎日1

「今、どこにいても、君のことばかり考えている。」

考えられないなんて、耐えられない。
許さなかった時間が、何気なく過ぎていく。

毎日 2

あなたが恋しくてたまりません。
今やあなたは私にとってすべてです。

記憶の中の遠いあなたへ

夜中に雨が降り、お酒を飲んでいると 習慣的にまたあなたのことを考え始めた。
まだ言っていない言葉、

記憶の中の遠いあなたへ。

やめたい

そんなふうに生きて、泣いたり笑ったり。

そんなふうに忘れられないなら仕方ない。

自分の中の小さな勝利に耐えられない。

君を知らない前に戻れるなら、

その時はそのまま通り過ぎたい。

やめたい。

やることにした

また考えたけど、結論が出なかった。

明日も明後日もたくさん考えようと思う。

停止ボタンを押した後、横になった。

何の準備もせずに、

やることにした。

それで私は、

「どうしたら深く愛せるだろうか？」
本を読んでいるときに、突然その考えが浮かんだ。
私は一日に何度も、何十回も彼女のことを考え、彼女の名前を呼ぶ。
私の愛の深さは本当にこんなに深いのだろうか？
その考えが突然浮かんだとき、私は彼女を探すために街へ出た。

彼女がどこにいるのか、何をしているのかわからず、私は無力に待っていた。
しかし、彼女はどこにも見つからなかった……。
だから私はあなたに電話したかった。

それでも、あなたはまだ

それでも、あなたはまだ、私の愛しい人。
たとえあなたが私に無関心でも、私が愛していた笑顔は今も変わらない
私の愛は私のそばにある

今、目を閉じるとそれを感じることができる。
私は一日中愛することだけを生きてきたから、それでいい。
私の心。

いつか、少し時間が経てば
またあなたとコミュニケーションがとれるようになる、
幸せに笑ってまたあなたに会えるようになる、
その日が来ることを願っている……。

その時、その時、私が持っているすべての愛をあなたに捧げます

どこにいるの

彼はどこにもいなかった。
彼が歩いたであろう距離を考え、
彼が座ったであろう同じ場所に座り、
私たちが交わした会話を思い出した。
私は静かに座り、チェリーエイドを一口飲んだ。
まるで彼が私の隣に座っているように感じた。
私に明るく微笑む彼の温かい笑顔……。
「あなたは私にとってすべてだった」と自分に言い聞かせている間、
まるで夢を見ているかのように、入間の「River flows in you」がイヤホンから流れてきた。

私はそんな終わりのない恋に落ちていたのかもしれない。

耐えられない何か

説明できない方法で私を閉じ込める言葉。

私から。

恋煩い 1

867、フリーダム・オブ・マインド、バン・テウォン

8670、サムタイムズ、ブリトニー・スピアーズ

86702、恋煩い、サンイー

恋煩い

恋煩い2

時間が経てば、すべては夢のように消え去る。
時間が経てば、すべては忘れ去られる。
心に深く刻んでおくと約束した記憶さえも
あなたを愛していたという事実さえも

フェードアウト

目を閉じて音楽を聞く。
頭の中で色々な考えが絡み合う。
音楽とともに時間が流れ、あの記憶へと連れ戻される。
何を言おうとしていたのか忘れてしまい、考えをまとめると、戻るボタンが押せなかったため曲が終わっていた。
過ぎてしまった時間は戻らないように、
割れたガラスの破片は元には戻らないように、

曲が終わると、記憶は消失点を超えて動き出す。
そうやって、
こうやって、
記憶は記憶から消えていく。

フェードアウト。
もう少しだけ近くに、私のそばに……。

2 小説のように

冬の雨｜私は待っています｜ティアラテ｜しかし、一つだけ確かなことは｜短縮ダイヤル1｜ラブレター｜春｜悲しい映画を見ているよう

冬の雨

初めて君を見たとき、君から目が離せなかった。

一目惚れするという言葉。

一目惚れするという言葉。以前は運命なんていう馬鹿げた言葉を信じていなかった。でも君に出会ってから変わった。君の声も、顔も、たまに吐く小さな息までも好きで、癖だと思うようになった。

君の声を頼りにたどり着いたカフェの前。君の好きな曲がここで流れていた。カフェの雰囲気が君の好みに似ていたからか？ それとも君の好きな曲を聞いたからか？ 今ここでどこかで君の声が聞こえてくる気がする。

聞き慣れた声と聞き慣れたメロディーのカフェに座り、妄想の中で君はモカコーヒーを飲み、僕はバナナシェイクを飲んでいた。

どこかで見たことがあるような、ある種のデジャブ現象のように、懐かしく感じた。まるで昔から君を知っていたかのように、とても心地よかった。君の温かい眼差し、明る

い笑顔、澄んだ瞳にきらめく美しい星。

そう、君はいつになく小さくて美しい星のようだ。君にそんなことを言ったっけ？

なぜ、その記憶は記憶から消えてしまうのだろう。

君を初めて見た日、運命だと思った。そして、悲しい恋に落ちて抜け出せない予感がした。

「何度言っても叫んでも、恋はいつか忘れてしまうもの……。僕よりも素敵な人に出会って幸せになってくれることを祈るよ。」

君の忘れてほしいという願いで、今こうして終わってしまった。

結局、記憶から忘れなければならない悲しい恋物語になってしまった。

「忘れることは本当に悲しいことだよ。」

私は待っています

その盲目で一方的な愛の終わりが決して美しくないことは
分かっていても、
私は待っています。
それを一度でもいいから見ることができたら。

ティアラテ

男：君を見ているこの瞬間が永遠に続くといいな。

女：はい？

男：（悲しそうな目で女を見て）ずっと君のそばに、ずっと、居て。

ストップモーションで状況が止まり、白黒画面に切り替わる。
時間が止まったようで、周囲は静まり返っている。

しかし、一つだけ確かなことは

夜が深まる。

言葉も表現もなく、未精製の思考だけが残る。

1、2、3、4、5、6、7、8、9、10、11、12、13、14、15、16、17、18、19、20

20秒後、感覚が湧き上がる。

しかし、未精製の感覚は内省を育まない。

思考で止まるものについても同じことが言える。

短縮ダイヤル1

彼はまだ考えずにはいられなかった。

彼女に会いたいときはいつでも、白い紙に彼女の名前を書いて、彼女のことを考えるしかなかった。

彼は白い紙に彼女の名前を書いた。「イ・グッスン、イ・グッスン」

すると、「ドゥルルク」、彼の携帯電話が振動した。

携帯電話は彼に貴重な情報を与えた。「今日、1000万ウォン借りられます」

彼は携帯電話を見て、短縮ダイヤル1を思い浮かべた。

それは彼女と連絡を取る唯一の方法であり、同時に大きな意味を持っていた。

彼は一瞬のうちにそのすべてを記憶から思い出した。

ラブレター

消しては書き直し、また消しては書き直し。
まだ後悔があるからやった。そして心の中に抑えきれない囁き、
今は記憶の彼方に、昔の話は悲しい旋律となり、私の体を包み込み、日常を揺さぶり、止まることなく一方通行で旅を続けている。
伝えたかった言葉が返ってきたある夜、私は夢を見た。その夢の中で、私はあなたを探してさまよっていた。
「今どこにいるの？ どこにいて何をしているの？ 元気にしてる？ よく食べて、よく寝て、そんな暮らしをしているの？ 不思議。全部。」 誰もいない、何もない場所で、私はそう叫んでいた。

いつから始まったの？ いつからあなたのことを考え始めたの？
私があなたに言った言葉は誠実ではなかったのか、それとも私の愛が真剣ではなかったからなのか？

春

長江気団の影響がなくなるまで。

シベリア気団の影響が終わった後、

北太平洋とオホーツク海気団の影響が出る前。

一年を四季に分けたときの最初の季節、

春。

悲しい映画を観ているような

私は愛しすぎた。
だから、私はすべてをあきらめた。
私でさえ、
これまでよく耐えてきた。
私は耐えられる。
今は……。

「愛は苦痛だ。愛は本当に苦痛だ。叶わない夢から目覚めると、部屋に一人でいるという事実が胸を痛める。心が空虚になり、今にも破裂しそうな愛。特に、盲目で片思いの場合。彼は女性と知り合い、恋に落ちた。ある日、彼は彼女の向かいに座って飲み物を飲みながら話をした。彼は、あの瞬間をどれほど美しく思い出し、夢見ていたか、そしてこのような瞬間がまた来るだろうか、このような瞬間が自分にも来るだろうかと考えた。すべては一瞬の夢に過ぎず、彼を閉じ込める言葉も一瞬で、通り過ぎる言葉もその

瞬間だけのものだ……。愛しましょう、辛いよ。ある日、彼は自分を振り返って、彼女に言うことが何もないことに気づき、シャワーを浴びて湯気の立った鏡を手のひらでこすったみすぼらしく惨めな自分の姿が見えました。彼はすべてを手放したかった。どこか遠くへ逃げ出したかった。彼女のことを考えている時間が心の中で止まり、その時間が永遠に続くことを願った。それが愛です。愛とは……。誰かを愛し、手を握り、軽くキスするだけでは愛ではありません。その人の成功を心から願っていても、その人と向き合って座って笑ったり話したりすることができなくても、一日中その人のことを考えて幸せに微笑んでいても、実現不可能な夢を見てまた悲しくなったとしても、それは愛です。いつかすべてが解決したとしても、この瞬間が永遠に続くことを願います。それができれば……。人が誰かを好きになることは間違っていません。結局、叶わなくても一日中愛して生きてきたからいいのだ。自分の気持ちをコントロールすることはできない。愛は彼を閉じ込め、理性的な判断を排除し、感情に振り回される。そう、彼は「愛」という牢獄に閉じ込められていた。過ぎ去る風のように時間が過ぎれば、大丈夫だろう。自分の気持ちさえもコントロールできない彼は、今、それを整理しようと

している。その時は本当に胸が張り裂けそうで悲しかったが、実際に過ぎ去れば、すべては無になるだろう？睡眠薬と水を飲めば、眠りに落ちる。目が覚めれば、何もなかったかのように、何もなかったかのように、心が楽になる。思春期の少年にとって、恋は熱病のように季節でもある。信じていたのにそうならなかったら、どうしようもない。ある日、彼は通りを歩いていると、店のショーウインドウに並べられた服を見て、「とてもきれいだ」と思った。「この服は彼女に似合うだろう。」いや、その時彼は頭の中で彼女にその服を買っていた。彼女はそれを着てくるりと回り、彼に明るい笑顔を向けた。しかし、それはすべて想像に過ぎなかった。彼と一緒にいた女性はどこにもいなかった。すべてが一瞬夢となり、映画館のスクリーンにはエンディングクレジットが流れていた。「悲しい映画を見たばかりのように、とても悲しくて胸が張り裂けそうだった。」

3
慰め

10年後｜ただ笑う｜若い顔1｜若い顔2｜ロンドンのスモッグ｜まるで最後みたい｜知らないこと｜未定の方向｜30歳、冬｜なし｜だから女はいつも悲しんでいる｜安らぎ｜理想｜眠れない｜第三者に拒否されました｜重要｜退屈だ｜いつも明るい｜希望

10年後

「弊社にご応募いただきありがとうございます。10年後のご自身について教えてください。」

「はい。10年後にはこの会社の専務取締役になりたいです。括弧を開けてお酒、括弧を閉じて専務取締役。」

（お酒）　専務取締役

ただ笑う

ただ笑う。

若い顔1

「1982年生まれで、今年30歳です。」
「えっ、本当ですか？ 若く見えますね。そんなに若くは見えませんよ。」
「ありがとうございます。若く見えます。何歳に見えますか？」
「1983年1月生まれで、29歳です。」

若き顔2

「なあ、今年で40歳になるんだけど、何歳に見える？」
「本当？ 若く見えるよ。」
「何歳に見える？」
「15歳、留年した中学1年生。」

ロンドンのスモッグ

うちの50歳のおばあちゃん、21歳で私を産んでからどれだけ苦労したの？
コメディアンのキム・グラの表現を借りれば、長男の現状はロンドンのスモッグみたいで、空は曇っている。
今は何も見えない。
若者の失業者数は120万人に迫り、ハイスペックな人たちが溢れているところで彼らと競争している。
でも、あまり心配しないで。
長男には無人島に落とされても生き残る粘り強さがある。
それは苦難と苦しみというものだ。
今は大変な時期が過ぎたので、これからの明るい未来だけを考えてください。

まるで最後みたい

卒業試験を受けて、
私の大学生活は実質終了です。
いつになったらまた学校に戻れるんだろう。

あちこち転々とした後、ようやく最終目的地にたどり着きました。
一生懸命勉強して、たくさんの人と遊び、
情熱を持って何かに向かって進んでいく

まるで夢だったみたいで、悔しい気持ちとほろ苦い気持ちが入り混じっています。

まるで最後みたい。

知らないこと

世の中には、知っているようで知らないことがたくさんある。
これから先、何が起こるのか、どんな性質を持つのか。
わからない。
わからない。

未定の方向

「今後はどうするつもりですか？」
カンギュが尋ねた。
「今は分からない。まだ何も決まっていないけど、まあ、今は漠然と先を見ているだけ。でも、どこにでも行けるよ。」
私は答えた。

30歳、冬

時間は待ってくれない、

何の準備もせずに30歳になる。

なし

これ以上の苦しみや悲しみなしに……。
そんなふうに生きられたらいいのに。

だから女はいつも悲しんでいる

女は言った。
「あなたから手紙をもらいたい。」
すると男は迷うことなく手紙を書き、女の細い白い手にそれを置いた。
きれいでも匂いもない粗末な手紙を受け取った女は男の前でそれを読み上げる。
「この手紙を読んだ人は24時間以内に同じメッセージを100人に送らなければなりません………。」

「あなたは愛を知らない。」
女は言った。

安らぎ

求職者はみな同じような感情を抱くのではないでしょうか？

最初はうまくやれると思っていたのに、失敗続きで疲れ果て、友達にも会えず、TOEICの本も置いてからずいぶん経ち、無力感と劣等感を感じながらただ横になったり、近所を散歩したりしています。

そう、痛みのない青春は青春として記憶されません。

いつかメリーJがこの瞬間を笑顔で思い出せる日が来ることを願っています。

理想

世俗的なことに縛られず、

小さなことでも満足し、感謝の気持ちを持つ人生

しかし、現実と理想はかけ離れています。

眠れない

眠れない。

嘘が真実を飲み込む暗い迷路をさまよう。

第三者に拒否されました

彼は彼女に尋ねました。

「どんな車に乗っていますか？ 中型車以上に乗っているはずです。初対面で年収を聞くのはちょっと気まずいです。車を見れば年収が推測できると思います。」

「はい、公共交通機関を利用します。よく歩きます。よく歩くので、「歩行者」と呼ばれています。」

「では、どこで働いていますか？ あ、会社より給料の方が大事です。ミレはいくら稼いでいますか？ 結局、物質的なものが現実です。あ、学歴も教えてください。TOEICの点数も知りたいのですが、聞くのは失礼だと思います。教えてくれたらメモします。」

「今は遊んでいるので、収入はありません。最高学歴は夜間学校卒業です。あ、でもTOEICの点数はあります。

「100くらいです。でも、なぜ私に聞くのですか？」

「ミレには未来がありません。残念ながら、あなたは私と友達になる条件を持っていません。私の友達に何か気持ち

があるなら、早くそれを乗り越えて自分の道を進んでください。ファイト。」
彼女は、当事者でもない、全く感情のない第三者に振られた。

その夜、ミレは何も考えずに面白いコメディ番組を見ながら大声で笑っていた。口の中で溶けていくポップコーンだけが彼女の気持ちを知っているような夜だった。

重要

誰もが一度は考えたことがあるでしょう。
私は他の人より遅れをとっているだろうか？
成績が悪いから、語学力が悪いから、容姿に自信がないから、勉強を始めるのが遅くて年を取っているから、大したキャリアがないから、などなど。
しかし、それは重要な問題ではありません。遅く始めてもいいのです。
もっと重要なのは、今どこにいるかではなく、
何を目標に定め、どこに向かっているかです。

私は自分の人生の正しい方向を定めているだろうか。
今、本当に重要なことを見逃していないだろうか？
「私は今どこに向かっているのか？」

退屈だ

「ああ、退屈だ。いつまで若者の恋愛話を聞かなきゃいけないんだ？ 退屈だ。退屈だ。」
「退屈だ。」

いつも明るい

この時点で就職や将来のことなど、不安や心配事はたくさんあるはずなのに、何も感じないし、感じない。
何も決まっていないし、進行中でもないし、進んでいるわけでもない。
考えずに生きているからなのかな？
そう、考えずに生きているから。
でも、まだ起こっていない未来のことを心配するより、今やったほうがいいのかもしれない。
やっぱりいいものはいい。
道を歩いているときに花屋に立ち寄って、花の匂いを嗅ぎながら、花屋さんに「この花、すごくいい匂いがする。花の名前は何？」と聞いた。
すると、店主は「造花だよ。」と言った。
風邪の匂いと勘違いしたんだろう。
最近はこんな些細なことで笑っちゃう。
そう、こうやって笑い続けていたら、いつかいい日が来る

んだろうな。

悲しいより悲しくないことのほうが好き。

希望

まだ暗くて薄暗いけど
いつか暖かい春が来る
そう、いつかいい日が来る
その希望とともに

いつかはこの瞬間も笑って思い出す思い出になると信じてる……。

4
ひどい愛

彼女と同じように、彼も｜君の風のように｜記憶の練習｜後になって後悔｜知らない｜後悔しないで｜送ってないよ｜愛しているけど、愛さない｜削除｜もし君の心が君が思っているよりもずっと大きいのなら｜悲しい歌や悲しい物話｜悲しい別れ｜見方を変えれば｜いつか会おうね｜昔の庭｜片付けなさい｜ひどい愛｜諦め｜混沌｜平行理論｜ホワイトアウト

彼女と同じように、彼も

「大丈夫。すべてうまくいく。」
彼女はそう言って、温かい手で彼を抱きしめた。しかし悲しいことに、彼の心の中で爆弾が爆発し、すべてが蜃気楼のように消え去った。
驚いて目を開け、腕時計を見ると、冷や汗が耳を伝っていた。

彼は再び安堵のため息をつき、再び横になった。
夢の中のもう一つの現実は、デジャブ現象のように思えた。
彼が心の中で時間を確認すると、理不尽な悲しみが胸にのしかかっていた。そして、彼女は彼の悲しい涙を拭い、「大丈夫。すべてうまくいく。」と言った。
そして、すべてが白い塵のように消え去った。
まるで夢の中で、彼が知らないうちに悠久の時間が過ぎ去ったかのように。

安定を見つけた彼の目が震え、光を見始めた瞬間、彼女は彼を見て悲しんでいた。

彼は彼女を温かい手で抱きしめ、「大丈夫。すべてうまくいく。」と言った。

君の風のように

暑い夏だった。
扇風機をつけて、
扇風機の前に立って「あー、あー、あー」と声を出した。

自然の風が顔に触れるたびに
「あー、あー、あー」と言った。

あー、静かに目を閉じて自然の風を感じ、そして自然に
いや、ゆっくりと、徐々に君を忘れていった。
君が望んだように
君の風のように

記憶の練習

かつては耐え難いと思われた愛は、

別れて他人になり

また他人になり

二人の間に何もなかったかのように忘れ去られる日が来る。

後になって後悔

「ずっと前から君のことが好きだったって言いたかったけど、うまくいかなかった。」

知らない

知ってる？ いや、知らない。知りたくない。今にも破裂しそうな私の心を知ることはできない。

後悔しないで

でも私は失望さえしていない。
この心の中で、愛の前で

雨の降る明洞の通りを歩くたびに、君を思う。
愛は雨に乗る
愛は音楽に乗る
ゆっくり、ゆっくり、速く、速く
ゆっくり、ゆっくり、速く、速く
そしてそれは終わる。

「後悔しないで。それは私が始めた愛だ。」

送ってないよ

「今、南部では今年最初のモンスーン雨が降り注いでいる。」

ラジオの天気予報を聞いていると、ふと君のことを思い出した。
別れた日に、最初のモンスーン雨が降った。

君の思いとともに、僕の中のすべてが溢れ出て、
あの日の記憶が消えていくように

記憶は消失点から遠ざかっていく。
でも、君の温かい声は、まだ僕の耳に残っている。
君が僕のもとを去ったのに、僕は君を心から離れなかったかのように。

忘れるのは一瞬だと人は言う。

僕は忘れたくない。

心の奥底にしまって、大切にしたい。

愛しているけど、愛さない

ワインを半分だけ注いでほしい。ワインの香りが優しく鼻腔をくすぐると、シャンソンを演奏できる。口の中がどんどん乾いていく、我慢できない。愛しい人よ、ジュテーム。物語はもう終わってしまったけれど、耐えられるだけの悲しみと、耐えられるだけの悲しみを感じさせてくれ、そうすればまた始められる。ワインを一口飲んだら、もう悲しくならないように、今すぐ行かせてくれ。

削除

深呼吸して吐き出します。

もう一度深呼吸して吐き出します。

全身がリラックスして快適になります。

全身がリラックスして快適になります。

全身の力が抜けて快適になります。

今、目の前にホワイトボードがあります。

ホワイトボードに愛する人の高画質写真が表示されます。

その人の写真がどんどん鮮明になります。

今、病んだ心を治す薬の封筒がその人の写真の上に表示されます。この薬の封筒の画像が鮮明になるにつれて、あなたの病んだ心は消えます。

今、1、2、3と数えると、あなたの病んだ心は癒されます。

1、

2、

3

今、あなたの病んだ心は癒されました。

黒板の前に黒板消しが表示されます。

黒板消しを使って、愛する人の写真を少しずつ消します。

今、1、2、3と数えると、その人の写真が白く消えます。

1、

2、

3

今、その人の写真は消されて消え去ります。

あなたの心はずっと軽くなります。

あなたの心はずっと軽くなり、楽になります。

あなたの心は楽になります。

もし君の心が君が思っているよりもずっと大きいのなら

もうこんなふうには生きていけない。
心を空っぽにしても、すぐにまたいっぱいになってしまう。

僕は君にとって
君は僕にとって

思い出のモザイクは一枚の写真、思い出のようなものだ。

数え切れないほどの時間が経てば、思い出は闇に消えていく。
もうこれ以上痛みや悲しみのないそんなふうに生きていければいいのに。

わからない。その時はどうしようもない。
もし君の心が君が思っているよりもずっと大きいのなら、

その時はどうしようもない。

耐えられない。

もうこんなふうには生きていけない。

一日に何度も君のことを考えてしまう。

もし君の心が君が思っているよりもずっと大きいのなら、

その時はどうしようもない。

もし君の心が君が思っているよりもずっと大きいのなら。

悲しい歌や悲しい物語

絵本に載ったことのない悲しい物語を聞いたり、初めて聞いた悲しいメロディーの歌手の声を聞いたりするとき、その時、私はあなたを思い浮かべます。

悲しい別れ

「これがすべて夢だったらいいのに。あなたをとても愛している。あなたを愛している。あなたをとても愛している。頭の先からつま先まであなたを愛している。あなたを愛している。あなたを愛している。あなたをとても愛している。頭の先からつま先まであなたを愛している。別れた翌日にまた笑って話せたらいいのに。」と私は思ったが、それは実現しなかった。いつもそうできるわけではないだろう。私は心からあなたを守り、愛したかった。やりたいことはたくさんあったのに、できなかったことを残念に思う。

「これがすべて夢だったらいいのに。」
でも、少なくとも一度は振り返ってほしいと思っていることを知っていますか？ それとも、知っているのに知らないふりをしますか？ 同じように感じたら、何もなかったかのように、何もなかったかのように、ただ笑って抱きしめて

ください。悲しくても、悲しまないでください。

「もう悲しい話は見られない。」

見方を変えれば

スターバックスのコーヒー一杯を買うには、工場でドリルで鉄に500個の穴を開けなければならない。

コーヒービーンのコーヒー一杯を買うには、工場でボルトを1000本締めなければならない。

締めたり掃除したり油をさしたりしてでも、あなたの心を掴みたい。

「こんなことをする人が好きな人がいる？」
「いや、そんな風に考えないで。この世には生計を立てることさえできない人がたくさんいる。それなのに、チョリョン、中型車に乗る余裕はないのか？ この世に、高貴な仕事と卑しい仕事の区別はどこにあるのか？ 他人に迷惑をかけずに正直に稼ぎ、倹約して貯金するのが一番だ。」

いつか会おうね

「ハニー、何してたの？」

「あなたのことを考えてたの。」

「ハニー、何してたの？」

「あなたのことを考えてたの。もう寝なきゃ。電話を切ろう。」

「ハニー、いつ会えるの？」

「いつか会おう。」

「ハニー、明日会える？」

「明日は忙しいの。」

「明後日はどう？」

「明後日も忙しいの。」

「じゃあ明後日はどう？」

「明後日も忙しいの。」

「じゃあいつ会えるの？」

「いつか会おうね、いいわ。」

「待つわ。」

昔の庭

喫茶店でアメリカーノを注文した後、窓の外を見ると、あなたに似た人がいました。何度もあなたに会いたかった。「この世にあの女性は一人だけ？ もう忘れてしまえ」。友達が慰めようとし、もう忘れてしまえと言ったとき、私は思わず腹を立てました。耳をふさいで、何も聞きたくありませんでした。今はどこにいても、あなたのことしか考えられません。「アメリカーノは好きだった？」 好きでした。好きだったかもしれません。確信から不確実性への思考の変化は、私があなたを忘れていることを思い出させました。その時、私は心が痛んで何を感じているのかわからず、何もできませんでした。長い時間が経ちました。長い時間が経ちました。古い思い出。古い悲しみ、古い忘れ、古い思い出。アメリカーノを飲むたびに、あなたのことを思い出します。今では、あなたは私の中のすべてになりました。あなたを忘れることはできないので、私はあなたを愛するだけです。

片付けなさい

「大丈夫。もし私を憎んでいると思うなら、正直に言って。もちろん、それは辛いだろうけど、私はそうする。私はただ心を空っぽにするだけ……。」

ひどい愛

愛して愛して、愛に笑い、愛に心を痛め、愛に微笑み、愛に悲しみ、愛に泣いて笑い、また愛して、愛に悲しんで傷つき、幸せになってまた愛してまた悲しむ。

ああ、ひどい愛。

諦め

本当に気持ち悪くて、汚くて、致命的で、不当です。
若い頃は、人生がこんなに難しくてつらいものだとは知りませんでした。

でも、どうしたらいいのでしょう？
まあ、そういう風に生きるしかないでしょうね。

混沌

ブラックホールのように君という名に囚われ、熱い感情が私の中で燃えている

抑えきれないこの心と感情を、
混沌とした愛と呼ぶ。

声に10デシベル加えて呼んでください。

混乱するよ。
すべて、
すべて、
一生愛すると決めた瞬間を破壊しなければならないこの感情。

平行理論

何度死んで生まれ変わっても、最後には君をまた愛するだろう。無限の軌道で数え切れないほど何度もまた会うだろう。姿も時間も違う運命のようにまた会って愛し合うだろう。磁石の北極が南極を探すように、僕の心も君を探すだろう。だから大丈夫。今は別れて、お互いの安否も知らずにこうして暮らしている。

今は電話もせず、メールもせず、熱烈な愛に胸が張り裂ける思いもしない。

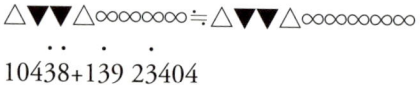

10438+139 23404

ホワイトアウト

またぐるぐる回ってしまう。

どれだけ頑張っても、失った感覚では君を見ることはできない。

君を近くに置きながらも、遠くをさまよう。

愛に目がくらみ、君の純白の心で。

また、また、もう一度、こうして。

僕は心を失う、

時間が止まる、

僕の記憶から君が消える、

愛は過ぎ去り、記憶は白い雪の中に消える。

忘れて、失って、忘れて、失って、忘れられて。

僕はまた自分の居場所を見つける。

5
会いたかったよ

温かい人｜プッシュしてロックを解除｜会いたかったよ｜電話を拒否｜オルフェウスの心｜主人公1と歩行者1

温かい人

カーテンを引いて窓を開けると、まぶしい日差しが部屋に入ってきました。
男は思いました。
「あなたは私にとってまぶしい人でした。ありがとう。ありがとう。あなたは私にとってとても温かい人でした。」

プッシュしてロックを解除

ある日、心が安らいだとき、
あなたを思い出す
[プッシュしてロックを解除]

会いたかったよ

「会いたかったよ。」

電話を拒否

女性はためらった後、男性に電話をかける。
「私はいつもあなたの一歩後ろにいたのに、あなたは私を決して見ないの? あなたが私を見て、手を振ってくれたら、私はいつもあなたを愛しています。」
ラブホリックの音楽の一部で構成されたクールな電話の呼び出し音が彼女の耳から消えると、「ただいま、お客様は電話に出ておりません」というメッセージが流れる。
女性は細い人差し指で終了ボタンを押しながら、「もうそんなことはしないほうがいいわ。」とつぶやく。
それは女性の愛が終わった瞬間だった。

オルフェウスの心

あなたは私の愛

あなたは私の運命

あなたは私の悲しみ

あなたのためなら何でもします。

愛に目がくらみ、

私の心は今も止まっています。

初めてあなたに会った時から今まで。

私の心の中にとどまって。

そして私はあなたのためにハープを弾きます。

あなたは目を閉じて、私が作曲した歌を聴いてください。

これはすべて夢に過ぎない、

この歌が終わってあなたが目を開けると、

この歌の中のすべてが一瞬で消えてしまいます。

そう、夢想家とはそういうものです。

この手でもう歌や言葉を書くことはできないようです。

でもあなたはまだ私の愛、

私の運命。

私は全身全霊であなたを愛します。

主人公1と歩行者1

弘大クラブ愛好家の中で2番目におっぱいが素敵な主人公1は、江南駅6番出口から徒歩5分ほどのニューヨークベーカリーの前で「バスキンロビンス31」というゲームに負けた罰として、歩行者1にジュエルキャンディリング（ジュエルキャンディ）を贈ってプロポーズした。
歩行者1は知り合って3分しか経っていない人のプロポーズを受け入れ、結婚して幸せに暮らした。

6
ファンタジー

私にはそれができる｜別れは美しく｜ファンタジー

私にはそれができる

「真剣さって何だか知ってる？ それは本当に真剣だった。もしそれが胸が張り裂けるような痛みであるなら、私は千回、一万回傷ついても幸せだ。ほんの一瞬、一度だけでもそれができたらどんなに素晴らしいだろうと思った。そんなに傷つくなら、私にはできると思った日があった。」

別れは美しく

#. 1126611

BGM: イルマの 「Love me」

全羅北道南原市広漢路の烏魯橋の中ほどで男女が出会う。

男:本気だ。春香を思い出すたびに胸がときめいて幸せだった。ありがとう。

女:モンリョンと別れなければならないと思うと胸が痛くなる。私の無数の欠点にもかかわらず、あなたが温かく接してくれて幸せだった。ありがとう。

ファンタジー

鏡の前には男がいる。

男の目には許されなかった時間が映っている。

時間の中で繰り広げられた幻想のすべてを君に話したくない。

残念だ。

あの扉を開けたらもう君に会えないような気がする。

幻想から目覚める時が来た。

さよならを言う時が来た。

さようなら。

まとめ

韻、音節、旋律を合わせ、リズムを出すことでしか詩の価値を高めることができないのは明らかです。しかし、私は別の方向で考えようとしました。無理やりまとめると、機械的に何かを踏みつぶすような感じがしたと言うべきでしょうか。変化のない単調さから抜け出したいと思いました。だから、最初に感じたように、そのまま表現しようとしました。

新しい方法で考えたかったのです。いつまでもアナログな思考に頼るわけにはいきませんでした。思いついた考えをメモ帳にペンで書き留めるだけでなく、スマートフォンの音声録音機能を使って見逃しやすい感情も捉えたかったのです。

より生き生きとした文章を書くために、すべてのものを新しい方法で見るようにしています。朝目が覚めた瞬間から夜寝るまで、作家のように考え、作家のように行動するようにしています。食事をするときも作家のように食べま

す。

これを新しい考えと変化と呼んでいます。今も、私の頭の中のメビウスの輪の中でパラダイムが変化し続けています。

そして記憶の中ですべての話が終わってしまった。